Contemporary Movie Hits 2nd Edition

ISBN 978-0-634-01581-6

7777 W. Bluemound Rd. P.O. Box 13819 Milwaukee, WI 53213

Visit Hal Leonard Online at
www.halleonard.com

ANYONE ELSE BUT YOU

from the Motion Picture Soundtrack JUNO

Words and Music by KIMYA DAWSON
and ADAM GREEN

G
but ___ you.
Female: Here is the church and here is the stee - ple. We
Cmaj7
G
sure are cute for two ug - ly peo - ple. I don't see what an - y - one can
Cmaj7
see in an - y - one ___ else ___ but ___
Male: We
G
Cmaj7
you.
both have shin - y hap - py fits of rage. ___ I want more fans, you

G
want more stage. I don't see what an - y - one can see in an - y - one
Cmaj7
G
else but you.
Female: You're al - ways try - in' to
Cmaj7
keep it real. And I'm in love with how you feel. I
G
Cmaj7
don't see what an - y - one can see in an - y - one else

G
but ___ you.
Male: I kiss you on the brain in the shad - ow of the train. ___ I
Cmaj7
G
kiss you all star - ry - eyed, my bod - y swings from side to side. I don't see what an - y - one can
Cmaj7
see in an - y - one else but ___
Female: The
G
Cmaj7
you.
peb - bles for - give me, the trees for - give me, and so why can't

G
you for - give me? I don't see what an - y - one can see in an - y - one
Cmaj7
G
else but you.
Male: Do do do do do do
Cmaj7
G
do do do do do, Both: do do do do do do do do do do do. I don't see what an - y - one can
Cmaj7
G
see in an - y - one else but you.

BELLA'S LULLABY

from the Summit Entertainment film TWILIGHT

Composed by CARTER BURWELL

8va
(8va)
(8va)
8va
dim.
pp
mp

mf
1.
sub. p
mp
2.

BENJAMIN AND DAISY

from THE CURIOUS CASE OF BENJAMIN BUTTON

By ALEXANDRE DESPLAT

D.S. al Coda
CODA
rit.

BREAKAWAY

from THE PRINCESS DIARIES 2: ROYAL ENGAGEMENT

Words and Music by BRIDGET BENENATE, AVRIL LAVIGNE and MATTHEW GERRARD

Am
G/B
C
Fsus2
Grew up in a small town and when the rain would fall down,
Am
G/B
Fsus2
I'd just stare out my win - dow.
Am
G/B
Dream-in' of what could be
C
Fsus2
Am
G
Fmaj7
and if I'd end up hap - py. I would pray.
Am
G/B
C
Fsus2
Try - ing hard to reach out but when I tried to speak out,
Wan - na feel the warm breeze. Sleep un - der a palm tree.

Am G/B Fsus2 Am G/B

felt like no one could hear ___ me. Want-ed to be-long here
Feel the rush of the o - cean. Get on-board a fast train.

C Fsus2 Am G

but some - thing felt so wrong here. So I'd
Trav - el on a jet plane far a -

Fsus2 Am G D

pray. (I would pray) I could break - a - way. ___
way ___ and break - a - way. ___

F G C G

I'll spread my wings and I'll learn how to fly. ___ I'll

Am
Fsus2
C
do what it takes 'til I touch the sky. I'll make a wish. Take a chance.
G
Am
G
Fsus2
Make a change and break - a - way.
C
G
Am
Out of the dark - ness and in - to the sun. But I won't for - get all the ones
Fsus2
C
G
To Coda
that I love. I'll / I got - ta take a risk. Take a chance. Make a change and

Am
G
Fsus2
Am
G/B
break - a - way.
Dah, dah, dah, dah, dah.
C
Fsus2
Am
G
Fsus2
D.S. al Coda
Dah, dah, dah, dah, dah.
Dah, dah, dah, dah, dah, dah, dah.
CODA
Am
G
Fsus2
G5
3fr
break - a - way.
Build - ing with a hun - dred floors.
C5
3fr
F5
G5
3fr
C5
3fr
F5
Swing-ing 'round re-volv - ing doors.
May-be I don't know where they'll
take me.
But,

G5
C5
F5
D5
got - ta keep mov - in' on, mov - in' on. Fly a - way, break - a -
F5
G5
C
G
way. I'll spread my wings and I'll learn how to fly.
Am
Fsus2
C
Though it's not eas - y to tell you good - bye, got - ta take a risk. Take a chance.
G
Am
G
Fsus2
Make a change and break - a - way.

C
G
Am
Out of the dark - ness and in - to the sun. But I won't for - get the
Fsus2
C
G
place I come from. I got - ta take a risk. Take a chance. Make a change and
Am
G
Fsus2
Am
G
break - a - way, break - a -
Fsus2
Am
G
Fsus2
way, break - a - way.

BREAKING FREE

from the Disney Channel Original Movie HIGH SCHOOL MUSICAL

Words and Music by
JAMIE HOUSTON

Cm F A♭

Male: You know the world can see ___ us ___ in a way that's dif -

E♭ B♭/D Cm F

- f'rent from who ___ we are. ___

Female: Cre - at - ing space be - tween ___ us, ___ till

A♭ E♭ B♭/D A♭

we're sep-'rate hearts. ___ *Both:* But your faith, ___ it gives ___

F7/A A♭(add2) E♭/A♭

___ me strength, ___ strength to ___ be - lieve. ___

Female: We're

Male: We're break- in' free. ___

Cm
F
A♭
soar - in', Male: fly - in'. Both: There's not a star in heav -
E♭
B♭/D
Cm
F
- en that we can't reach. Male: If we're try - in', Both: yeah, we're break -
A♭
A♭maj7(no3)
A♭
A♭maj7(no3)
Cm
in' free. Male: Oh, we're break - in' free. Can you feel it build -
F
A♭
E♭
B♭/D
- ing, like a wave the o - cean just can't con - trol,

Cm
F
A♭
Female: con-nect-ed by a feel - in', oh, in our ver - y souls,
E♭
B♭/D
A♭
F7/A
ris - ing till it lifts us up so
A♭
A♭(add2)
Cm
ev - 'ry - one can see?
Female: We're soar - in', Male: fly -
Female: Run - nin', Male: climb-
Male: We're break - in' free.
F
A♭
E♭
B♭/D
- in'. Both: There's not a star in heav - en that we can't reach.
- in', Both: to get to that place to be all that we can be.

Cm
F
A♭
A♭maj7(no3)
Male: If we're try - in', Both: yeah, we're break - in' free. Male: Oh, we're break -
Male: Now's the time, Both: so we're break - in' free. Male: We're break -
1
A♭
A♭maj7(no3)
in' free.
2
E♭
B♭/D
A♭
in' free. More than hope, more than faith,
F7/A
A♭
Female: this is truth, this is fate; and to - geth - er, we see
Both:
it com - in'. Male: More than you, more than me, Female: not a want, but a need:
F7/A

A♭
4fr
Dm
N.C.
Dm
N.C.
G
Both: both of us break-in' free.
Female: Soar - in',
Male: fly -
B♭
F
C/E
- in'.
Both: There's not a star in heav - en that we can't reach.
Dm
G
B♭
If we're try - in', yeah, we're break - in' free.
Break - in' free.
Dm
G
Female: We're run - nin',
Male: ooh, climb - in'
Both: to

B♭
F
C/E
Dm
get to the place to be all that we can be. Now's the time,
G
B♭
Female: so we're break - in' free.
Male: Oh, we're break - in' free.
Dm
G
B♭(add2)
3fr
You know the world can see us in a way that's
rit.
F
C/E
B♭maj9
5fr
dif - f'rent from who we are.
8va

BY THE BOAB TREE

from the Twentieth Century Fox Motion Picture AUSTRALIA

Written by BAZ LUHRMANN,
FELIX MEAGHER, ANGELA LITTLE,
ANTON MONSTED and SCHUYLER WEISS

* *Lead vocal written an octave higher than sung.*

Cm
D7
D
G
D(add4)/F♯
Now I know you're some - where. You're ev - 'ry - where to me,
Em7
D(add4)
Csus2
C6
a whis - per on the breeze, the earth be - neath my feet.
G
D6
Am7/D
G
D(add4)/F♯
And when the rain falls down, you tell a
Em7
D(add4)
Csus2
C6
sto - ry, and I will hear you, al - ways

G D6 Am7/D G C5 3fr G C C/D
near you, by the bo-ab tree. The
G C G C
land will hold its se - crets to whis - per on the wind. The
Em7 A Am7 Dsus D
rain will fall, the grass grow green, and life be - gins a - gain. And
G C Cm 3fr D7 D
I will nev-er be a - fraid. Now I know you're

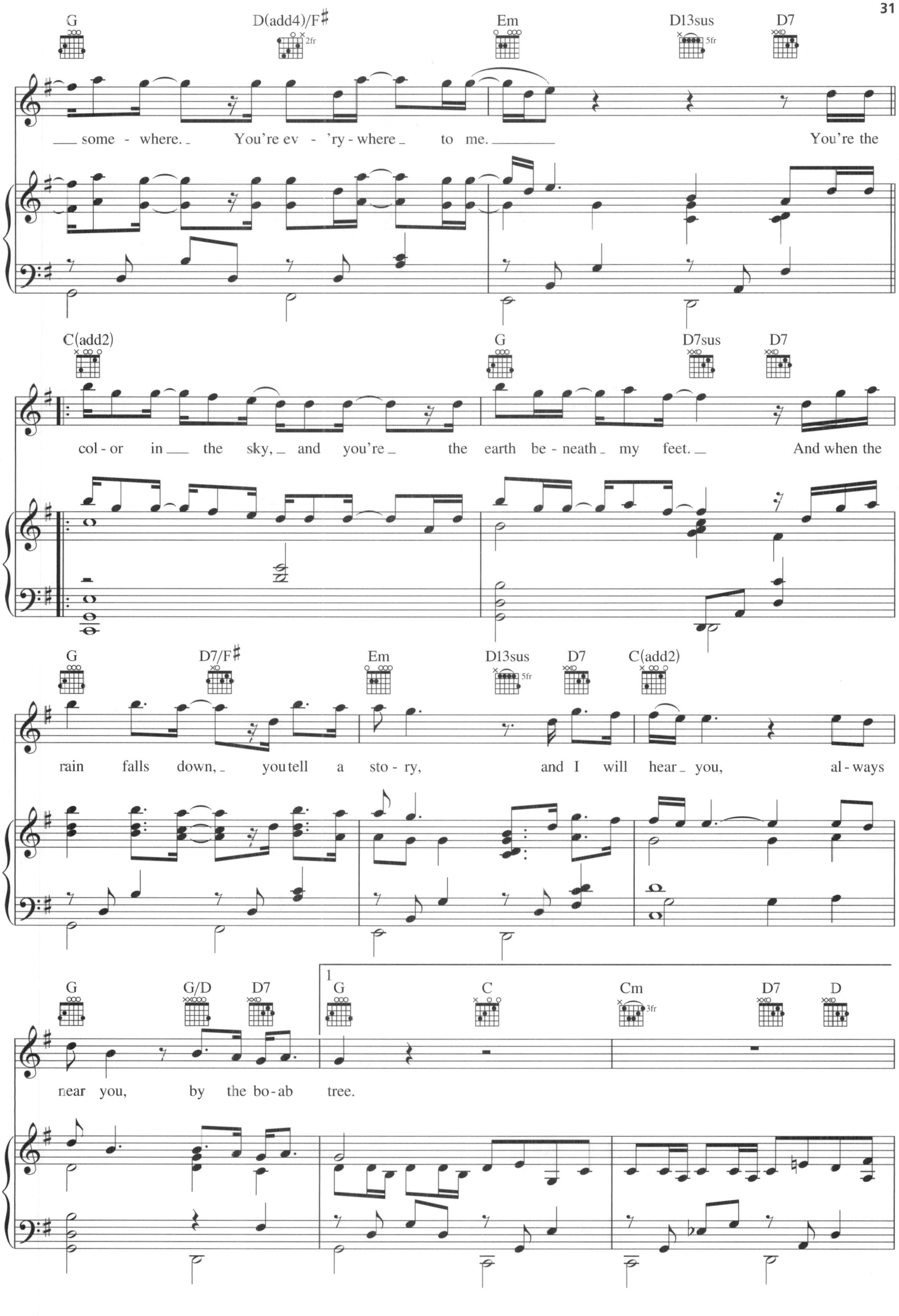

G D(add4)/F♯ Em D13sus D7

some - where. You're ev - 'ry - where to me. You're the

C(add2) G D7sus D7

col - or in the sky, and you're the earth be - neath my feet. And when the

G D7/F♯ Em D13sus D7 C(add2)

rain falls down, you tell a sto - ry, and I will hear you, al - ways

G G/D D7 1 G C Cm D7 D

near you, by the bo - ab tree.

G
D/F♯
Em
G/D
Csus2
G/B
G/C
D7
3fr
G
G/B
G/C
D7
G
D(add4)/F♯
2fr
Oh, you are some - where; you're ev - 'ry - where to me.
Em
D13sus
D7
5fr
2
G5
3fr
C
C6
G
C
You're the tree.
G
C6
G
Cmaj9
C(add2)
C
C6
G5
3fr
rit.

CAN I HAVE THIS DANCE

Walt Disney Pictures Presents HIGH SCHOOL MUSICAL 3: SENIOR YEAR

Words and Music by ADAM ANDERS
and NIKKI HASSMAN

C
C/B
eyes locked on mine, and let the
Fsus2
G(add4)
mu - sic be your guide. Troy: Won't you
Am7
C/F
3fr
Gsus
3fr
prom - ise me we'll keep
Gabriella: (Now won't you prom - ise me that you'll nev - er for - get
Am7
F
B♭
danc - ing, wher - ev - er we go next? Both: It's
to keep danc - ing, wher - ev - er we go next?)

C
C/D
C/E
like catch - ing light - ning, the chanc - es of find - ing some-one
Fmaj9
G
Gsus
3fr
C
like you. It's one in a mil -
C/D
C/E
Fmaj9
- lion, the chanc - es of feel - ing the way
G
Am7
C/F
3fr
we do. And with ev - 'ry

G
Am7
C/F
3fr
step to - geth - er, we just keep on
G
B♭(add2)
3fr
get - ting bet - ter. Gabriella: So can I have this dance?
Troy: (Can I have this dance?)
Csus
3fr
C
To Coda
Both: Can I have this dance?
Csus2
3fr
C
C/B
Troy: Take my hand; I'll take the lead,

Fsus2
Gsus
and ev - 'ry turn will be safe with me.
C
C/B
Don't be a - fraid, a - fraid to fall.
Fsus2
G(add4)
You know I'll catch you through it all.
Am7
C/F
Gsus
And you can't keep us a - part,
Gabriella: (E - ven a thou - sand miles can't

Am7 F B♭

'cause my heart is wher - ev - er you
keep us a - part, 'cause my heart is wher - ev - er you

D.S. al Coda

are. *Both:* It's
are.)

CODA

Csus2 C Gm7

Gabriella:
Oh, no moun - tain's too

B♭(add2) Dm7

high, and no *Both:* o - cean's too wide, 'cause to - geth - er or not,

B♭(add2)
3fr
Dm7
pour; what we have is worth fight-ing for. You know I be-lieve
B♭
B♭maj7(no3)
B♭6
that we were meant to be,
B♭sus2
C
C/D
yeah. It's like catch-ing light-ning, the chanc-es of find-
C/E
Fmaj9
G
-ing some-one like you.

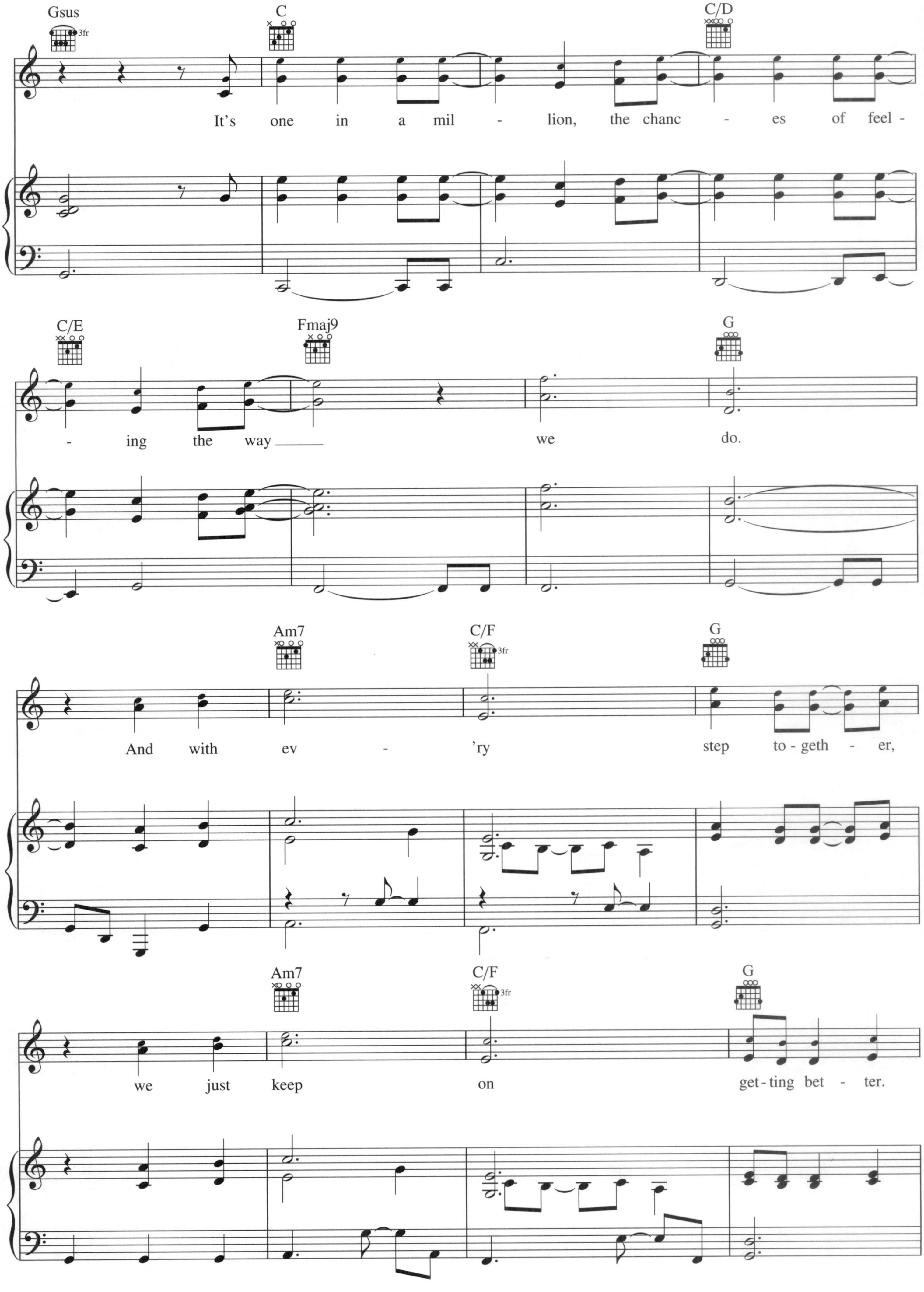
Gsus
C
C/D
3fr
It's one in a mil - lion, the chanc - es of feel -
C/E
Fmaj9
G
- ing the way we do.
Am7
C/F
G
3fr
And with ev - 'ry step to-geth - er,
Am7
C/F
G
3fr
we just keep on get-ting bet - ter.

B♭(add2)
3fr
Troy: (Can I have this dance?)
Gabriella: So can I have this dance?
Both: Can
Csus
3fr
C
Csus2
3fr
I have this dance?
Gabriella: Can
C
B♭
C/B♭
B♭
Both:
I have this dance?
Can I have this
Csus
3fr
C
Csus2
3fr
C
dance?

DAWN
from PRIDE AND PREJUDICE

By DARIO MARIANELLI

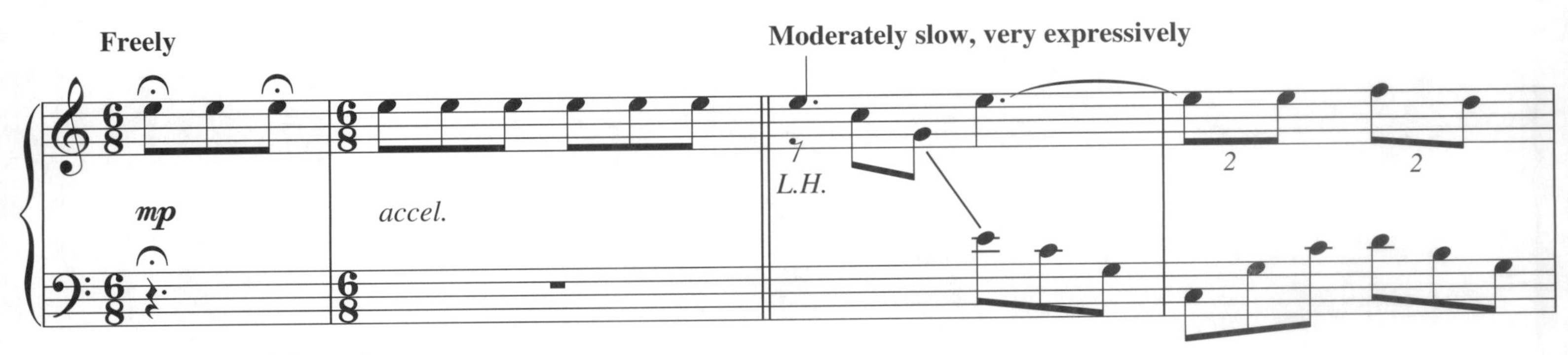

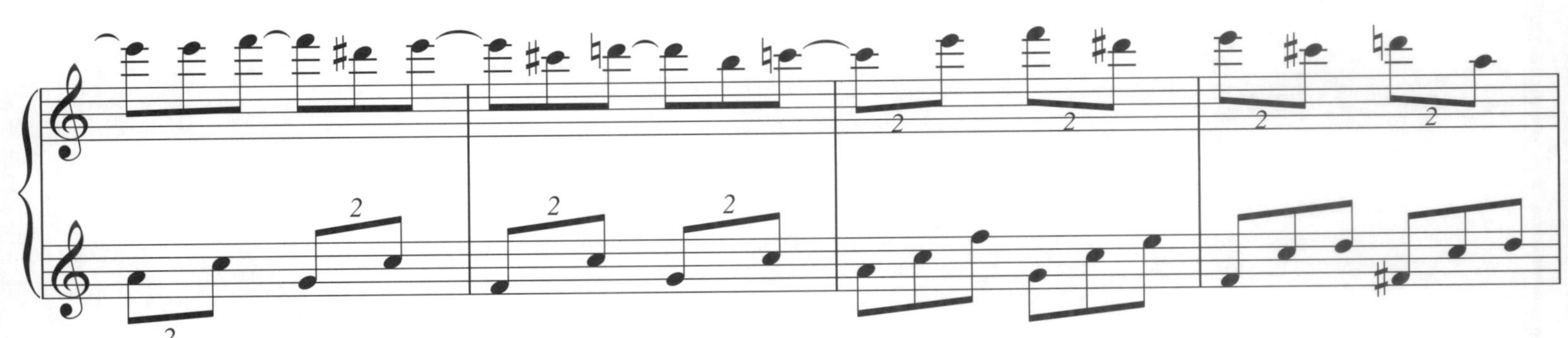

Moderately fast, with motion
rit.

Slightly slower

rit.
Slowly
8va
(8va)
rit.

I THOUGHT I LOST YOU

from Walt Disney Pictures' BOLT

Words and Music by MILEY CYRUS
and JEFFREY STEELE

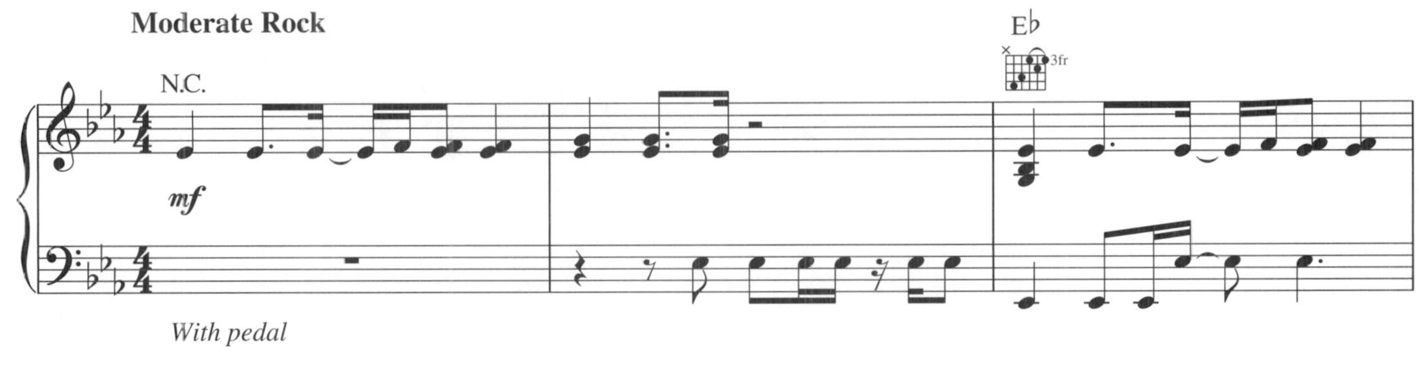

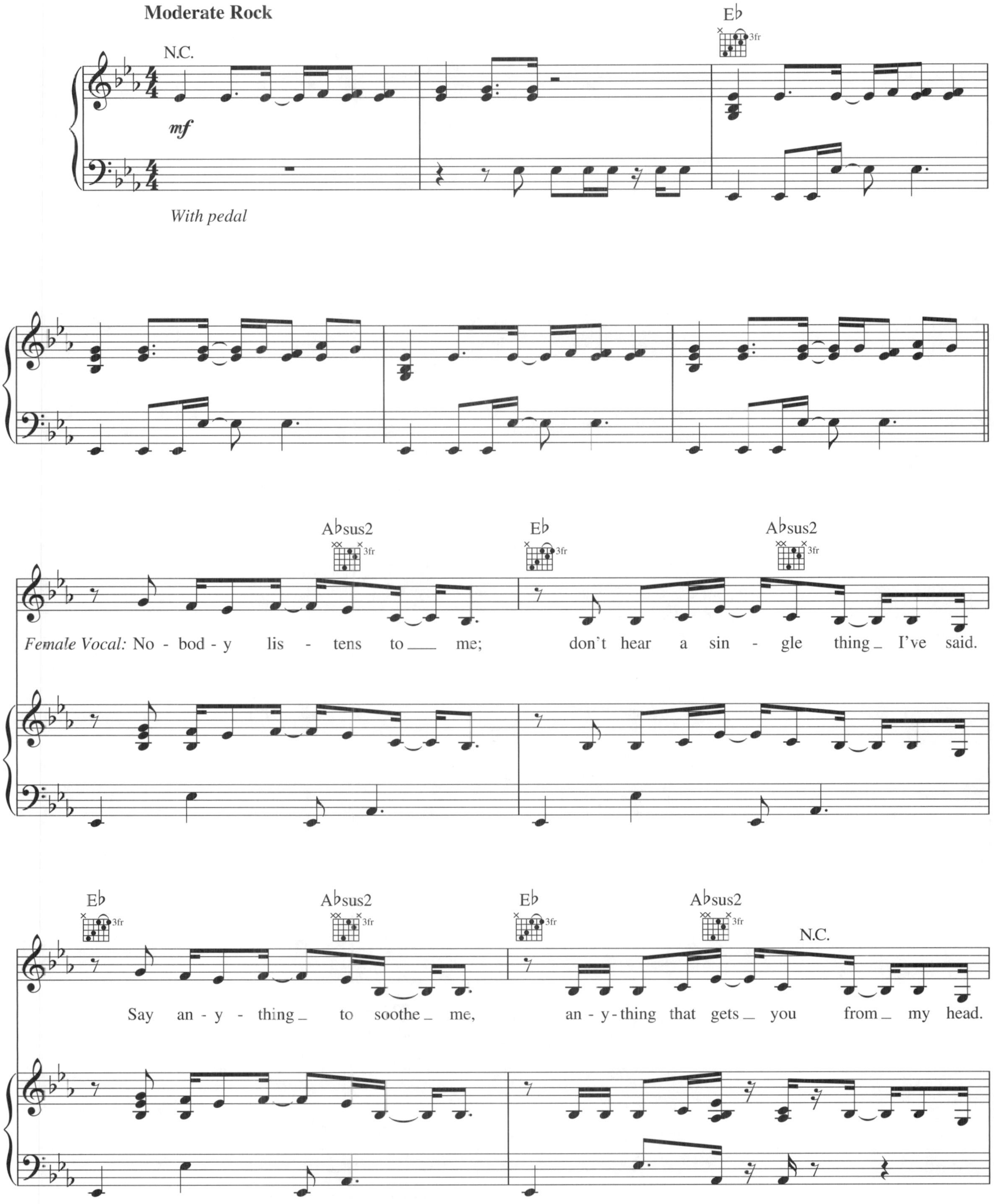
Moderate Rock
N.C.
E♭
mf
With pedal
A♭sus2
E♭
A♭sus2
Female Vocal: No - bod - y lis - tens to ___ me; don't hear a sin - gle thing _ I've said.
E♭
A♭sus2
E♭
A♭sus2
N.C.
Say an - y - thing _ to soothe _ me, an - y - thing that gets _ you from _ my head.

Eb
Absus2
3fr
Don't know how I real - ly feel; I fake the daze to make like I don't care.
Don't know how much it hurts; I turn a - round like you were nev - er there.
Fm7(add4)
Ebmaj7/G
Ab5
Eb/G
4fr
N.C.
Like some-how, you could be re - placed,
Ab
and I could walk a - way from the prom - is - es we made and

E♭
Fm7(add4)
Male:
Female:
swore we'd nev - er break.
I thought I lost you when you
A♭sus2
B♭(add4)
ran a - way to try to find me;
I thought I'd nev - er see your
sweet face a - gain.
I turned a - round and you were gone,
and on and on the days went.
Cm
I kept the mo - ment that

A♭
E♭
Cm
we were in,
'cause I hoped in my heart you'd come
B♭/D
E♭
Fm7(add4)
E♭/G
A♭sus2
B♭sus
back to me, my friend. And now I got you;
Cm B♭(add4)/D E♭
Fm7(add4)
E♭
To Coda
but I thought I'd lost you.
E♭
A♭sus2
E♭
A♭sus2
Male: I felt so emp - ty out there,
and there were days I had my doubts.

E♭
A♭sus2
E♭
A♭sus2
But I knew I'd find you some-where, be-cause I knew I could-n't live with-out
Fm7(add4)
E♭maj7/G
A♭5
E♭/G
N.C.
A♭5
E♭/G
N.C.
you in my life for one more day.
Fm7(add4)
E♭maj7/G
A♭
Male:
Female:
D.S. al Coda
And I swore I'd nev-er break those prom-is-es we made.
CODA
Cm
N.C.
B♭/D
Male: I told my-self I would-n't sleep till I

E♭
3fr
N.C.
Fm
Gm
3fr
N.C.
Fm
Gm
3fr
N.C.
Fm
searched the world from sea to sea.
Female: I
Cm
3fr
N.C.
B♭/D
E♭
3fr
N.C.
Fm
Male:
made a wish up - on a star; I turn a - round, and there you were. Now
Fm7(add4)
E♭maj7/G
E♭/A♭
6fr
B♭7sus
here we are, are.
Female: Here we are.
E♭
3fr
Fm7(add4)
A♭sus2
3fr
I thought I lost you.
Male: I thought I lost you, too.

E♭
Fm7(add4)
A♭5
E♭/G
N.C.
A♭5
E♭/G
N.C.
I thought I lost you.
Yeah.
I thought I lost you.
E♭
Fm7(add4)
A♭sus2
B♭(add4)
Male:
Female:
I thought I lost you when you ran a-way to try to find me;
E♭
Fm7(add4)
A♭sus2
B♭(add4)
I thought I'd nev-er see your sweet face a-gain.
E♭
Fm7(add4)
A♭sus2
B♭(add4)
I turned a-round and you were gone, and on and on the days went.

Cm
3fr
A♭
4fr
E♭
3fr
I kept the mo - ment that we were in,
Cm
3fr
B♭/D
E♭
3fr
'cause I hoped in my heart you'd come back to me, my friend. And now I got
Fm7(add4)
E♭/G
A♭sus2
B♭sus
Cm
B♭(add4)/D
E♭
Fm7(add4)
E♭
A♭sus2
you;
but I thought I lost you.
E♭
A♭sus2
E♭
A♭sus2
Female: But I thought I lost you.
Male: I thought I lost you, too.

E♭
A♭sus2
E♭
A♭sus2
Male:
Female:
So glad I got you, got you.
E♭
A♭sus2
E♭
A♭sus2
Female: So glad I got you, yeah, yeah.
E♭
A♭sus2
E♭
I thought I
lost you.
Male: I thought I lost you, too.

HE'S A PIRATE

from Walt Disney Pictures' PIRATES OF THE CARIBBEAN: THE CURSE OF THE BLACK PEARL

Music by KLAUS BADELT

8vb
8vb
8vb

8vb
(8vb)

I WALK THE LINE

Words and Music by
JOHN R. CASH

Additional Lyrics

3. As sure as night is dark and day is light,
   I keep you on my mind both day and night.
   And happiness I've known proves that it's right.
   Because you're mine I walk the line.

4. You've got a way to keep me on your side.
   You give me cause for love that I can't hide.
   For you I know I'd even try to turn the tide.
   Because you're mine I walk the line.

5. I keep a close watch on this heart of mine.
   I keep my eyes wide open all the time.
   I keep the ends out for the tie that binds.
   Because you're mine I walk the line.

LEARN TO BE LONELY

from THE PHANTOM OF THE OPERA

Music by ANDREW LLOYD WEBBER
Lyrics by CHARLES HART

E♭/B♭ F Dm Dsus Dm Gsus(add2) Gm Gsus(add2) Gm Csus Cm
care for you? Learn to be lone - ly. learn to be your
Cm7 E♭/F F B♭ Cm/B♭ F9
one com - pan - ion. Nev - er dream that out in the world there are arms to
B♭6 B♭ Gm Gm6 D A9
hold you. You've al - ways known your heart was on its
F7 B♭ B♭maj7 Cm/B♭ F
own. So laugh in your lone - li - ness.

Bb
Cm/Bb
F
Dm
Dsus
Dm
Child of the wil - der- ness. Learn to be
Gsus(add2) Gm Gsus(add2) Gm
Csus
Cm
Cm7
F7b9
Bb
Bbmaj7
lone - ly, learn how to love life that is lived a - lone.
Cm/Bb
F
Bb
Bbmaj7
Cm/Bb
F
Dm
Dsus
Dm
Learn to be
Gsus
Gm
Csus
Cm
F7b9
Bb
lone - ly. Life can be lived, life can be loved a - lone.
p
rit.
pp

LISTEN

from the Motion Picture DREAMGIRLS

Music and Lyrics by HENRY KRIEGER, ANNE PREVEN,
SCOTT CUTLER and BEYONCÉ KNOWLES

* Recorded a half step higher.

Cm7
3fr
F7sus
F
only be - gin - ning _ to find re - lease. Oh, the
one I thought _ had died _ so long a - go. Oh, I'm
D♭
F7/A
3fr
B♭m7
Fm7
time has come for my dreams to be heard. They will not be pushed a - side and turned
scream - ing out, and my dreams will be heard. They will not be pushed a - side, or worse,
G♭
G♭6
F7sus
F
F7sus
in - to your own, all 'cause you won't lis - ten. ___
B♭
F/A
Lis - ten: I am a - lone at a cross - roads. I'm not at home in my

Gm
F6
E♭
Dm7
own home, and I've tried and tried _ to say what's on my mind. You should have known.
B♭
F/A
Oh, now I'm done be-liev - ing you. ___ You don't know what I'm feel - ing. I'm
E♭maj7
F/E♭
D/F♯
Gm
more than what _ you made of me. ___ I fol-lowed the voice _ you gave to me, ___
1
Cm7
F7sus
but now I've got - ta find ___ my own. ___ You should have

2
Cm7
3fr
F7sus
D♭
F7/A
3fr
but now I've got - ta find my own.
I don't know where I be - long, but
Bbm7
Fm7
G♭
I'll be mov-ing on.
If you don't, if you
F7sus
B♭
F/A
won't,
lis - ten to the
Gm
3fr
D/F♯
Cm7
3fr
song here in my heart,
a mel - o - dy I start, but I

F7sus
Bb
will com - plete.
Oh, now I'm done be - liev - ing you.
F/A
Ebmaj7
F/Eb
You don't know what I'm feel - ing. I'm more than what you made of me. I
D/F#
Gm
F6
Cm7
fol-lowed the voice you think you gave to me. But now I've got - ta find my
F7sus
F
Bb
own, my own.
3fr
8vb
Ped.

MAMMA MIA

from MAMMA MIA!

Words and Music by BENNY ANDERSSON, BJÖRN ULVAEUS and STIG ANDERSON

G
D
Look at me now,
D+
D
D+
will I ev - er learn? I don't know how,
but I sud - den - ly lose
G
A
con - trol.
There's a fire with - in my soul.
G D A
G D
Just one look and I can hear a bell ring.
One more

A
look and I for - get ev - 'ry - thing,
oh,
oh.
D
Mam - ma Mi - a,
here I go a - gain.
G
C/G
G
D/G
D
My, my how can I re - sist ya?
G
C/G
G
Mam-ma Mi - a,
does it show a - gain,
my, my, just

D/G
D
A/C♯
how much I've missed ya?
Yes, I've been bro - ken - heart - ed,
Bm
A6
G
C
G
Em7
blue since the day we part - ed.
Why, why did
A
D
Bm
To Coda
I ev - er let you go?
Mam-ma Mi - a,
now I real - ly know,
G
C
G
Em7
1
A
D+
my, my,
I should not have let you go.

D
D+
2
A
D
D+
should not have let you go.
DONNA: What the hell are you all doing here?
D
D+
Well, I'd love to stop and chat, but I have to go and clean out my handbag or something.
G
Gmaj7
BILL: Age does not wither her.
HARRY: I was expecting a rather stout matron.

A6
A
G
D
SAM: No, she's still Donna.
Just one
A
G
D
look and I can hear a bell ring.
One more
A
D.S. al Coda
look and I for - get ev - 'ry - thing,
oh, oh.
CODA
G
C
G
Em7
A
D
my, my, I should not have let you go.

SPIDER PIG

from THE SIMPSONS MOVIE

Based on the composition "Theme from Spiderman"
written by PAUL FRANCIS WEBSTER and BOB HARRIS
Parody Lyrics by JAMES I. BROOKS,
MATT GROENING, AL JEAN, IAN MAXTONE GRAHAM,
GEORGE MEYER, DAVID MIRKIN, MIKE REISS,
MIKE SCULLY, MATT SELMAN,
JOHN SWARTZWELDER and JON VITTI

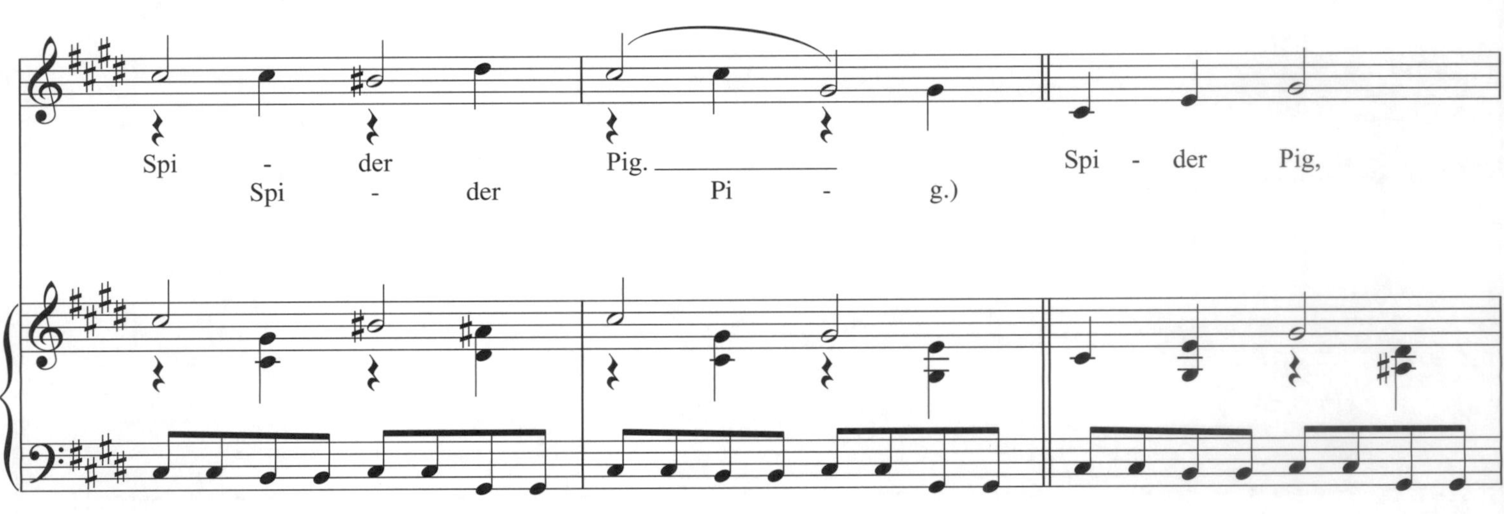

F#m
spi - der pig does.
Can he swing
(Oh, can he
C#5
from a web?
swing from a web? Oh
No he can't;
no, he's a
A G# N.C. F#m/A D#7sus G#7#5 F#m6 G#7 G#7#5
he's a pig.
pig.) (Look out! He is a spi - der,
He is a spi - der
N.C.
pig.
Spi - der Pig.)
A G# F#m/A D#7sus
(Look out! He is a

G♯7♯5
F♯m6
G♯7
G♯7♯5
4fr
4fr
4fr
N.C.
He is a spi - der pig.
spi - der, Spi - der
Pi - g.)
Oh,
(Spi - der Pi - g.
Spi - der Pig.
Spi - der Pi - g.
Oh,
Spi - der
Pi - g.)
Spi - der Pig.

'TIL HIM
from THE PRODUCERS

Music and Lyrics by
MEL BROOKS

D7
Gm
3fr
Cdim7/G
4fr
G7sus
G7
C7
chance, then I felt his mag - ic and my heart be - gan to dance!
Gm7/C
C13
2fr
F
B♭/F
C7
Fmaj7
I was al - ways fright - ened, fraught with wor - ry 'til him.
mp
C7/F
F(add9)
C7/F
Am7♭5
I was go - ing no-where in a hur - ry 'til him.
D7
B♭
Gm7♭5
He filled up my emp - ty life,
5
f

Am7 Am7/D D7 G7sus G7 B♭/C Gm7♭5/C

filled it to the brim. There could nev - er ev - er be an - oth - er one like

poco rit. *mp* a tempo poco rit.

F C7 F F♯m7/B

him.

B9 E A/E B7/E

MAX:

No one ev - er ev - er real - ly knew me 'til

mp

E(add9) A/E B7 E B7/E B7/A

him. Ev - 'ry - one was al - ways out to screw me 'til

G♯m7♭5
C♯7♭5
8fr
C♯7
F♯m7
him.
Nev - er met a man I ev - er
B7
G♯m7
4fr
C♯7
trust - ed,
al - ways dealt with shy - sters in the past.
F♯m7
Fdim7
F♯7sus
F♯
B7sus
2fr
Now I'm well - ad - just - ed
'cause I've got a friend at
last.
poco rit.
A tempo
B9
C9
Fmaj7
B♭/F
C7/F
Al - ways play - ing sin - gles, nev - er
dou - bles
'til
poco rall.
mp

F
B♭/F
C/F
3fr
F(add9)
C7/F
him.
Nev - er had a pal to share my trou - bles 'til
Am7♭5
D7
Gm7
B♭m
LEO & MAX:
him.
He filled up my emp - ty life,
f
Am7
Am7/D
D7
G7sus
G7
Gm7♭5
LEO:
filled it to the brim.
There could nev - er ev - er be an - oth - er one
poco rit.
a tempo
poco rit.
Slowly
F
B♭/F
F(add9)
like him.

THAT'S HOW YOU KNOW

from Walt Disney Pictures' ENCHANTED

Music by ALAN MENKEN
Lyrics by STEPHEN SCHWARTZ

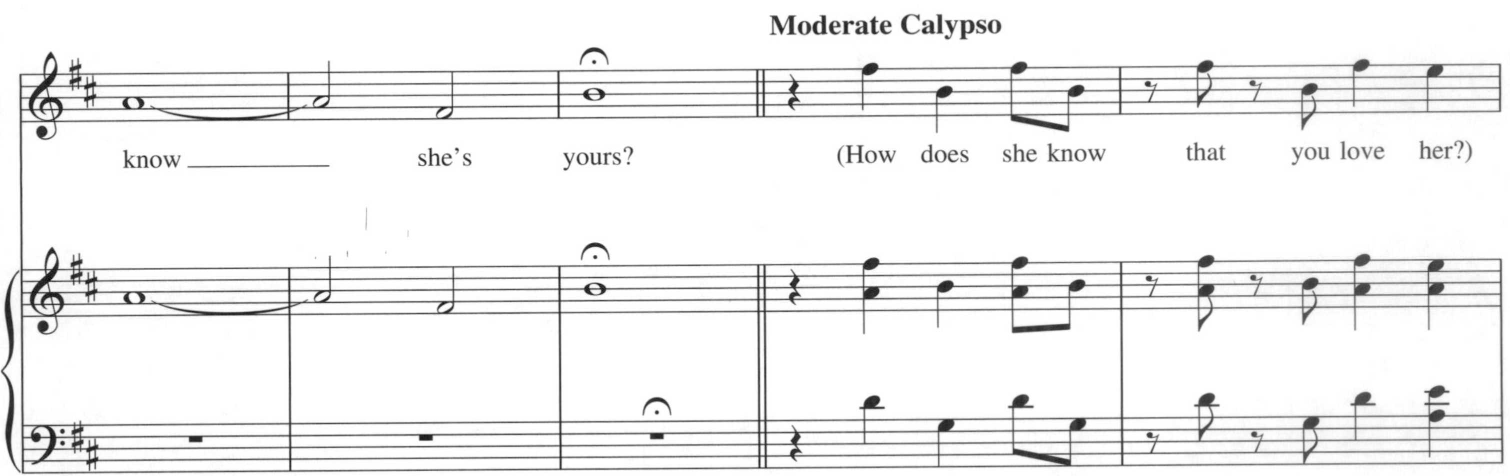

How does she know that you real - ly... real - ly... tru - ly... love her?
How does she know that you love her? How do you show her you love her?
F#7
B
E
G
A
How does she know that you real - ly, real - ly, tru - ly love her?
D
G/D
D/A
A
D
G/D
It's not e - nough to take the one you love for grant - ed.

Em
A
D
G/D
A
F♯
You must re - mind her, or she'll be in - clined to
B
B/D♯
4fr
E
Emaj7/G♯
G/A
3fr
A7
D
G/D
Em7
say: "How do I know
G/A
3fr
A7
D
G/D
Em7
G/A
3fr
A7
he loves me? How do I
D
G/D
Em7
F♯7sus
F♯7
B
B/D♯
4fr
G♯m
4fr
know he's mine?"

B E F♯ B B/D♯ E
Well, does he leave a lit - tle note to tell you you are
C♯m7 C♯m7/F♯ F♯7 B B/D♯
on his mind? Send you yel - low flow - ers
E C♯m7 C♯m7/F♯ F♯7
when the sky is gray? Hey.
D♯m G♯m B/C♯
He'll find a new way to show you a lit - tle bit ev - 'ry day.

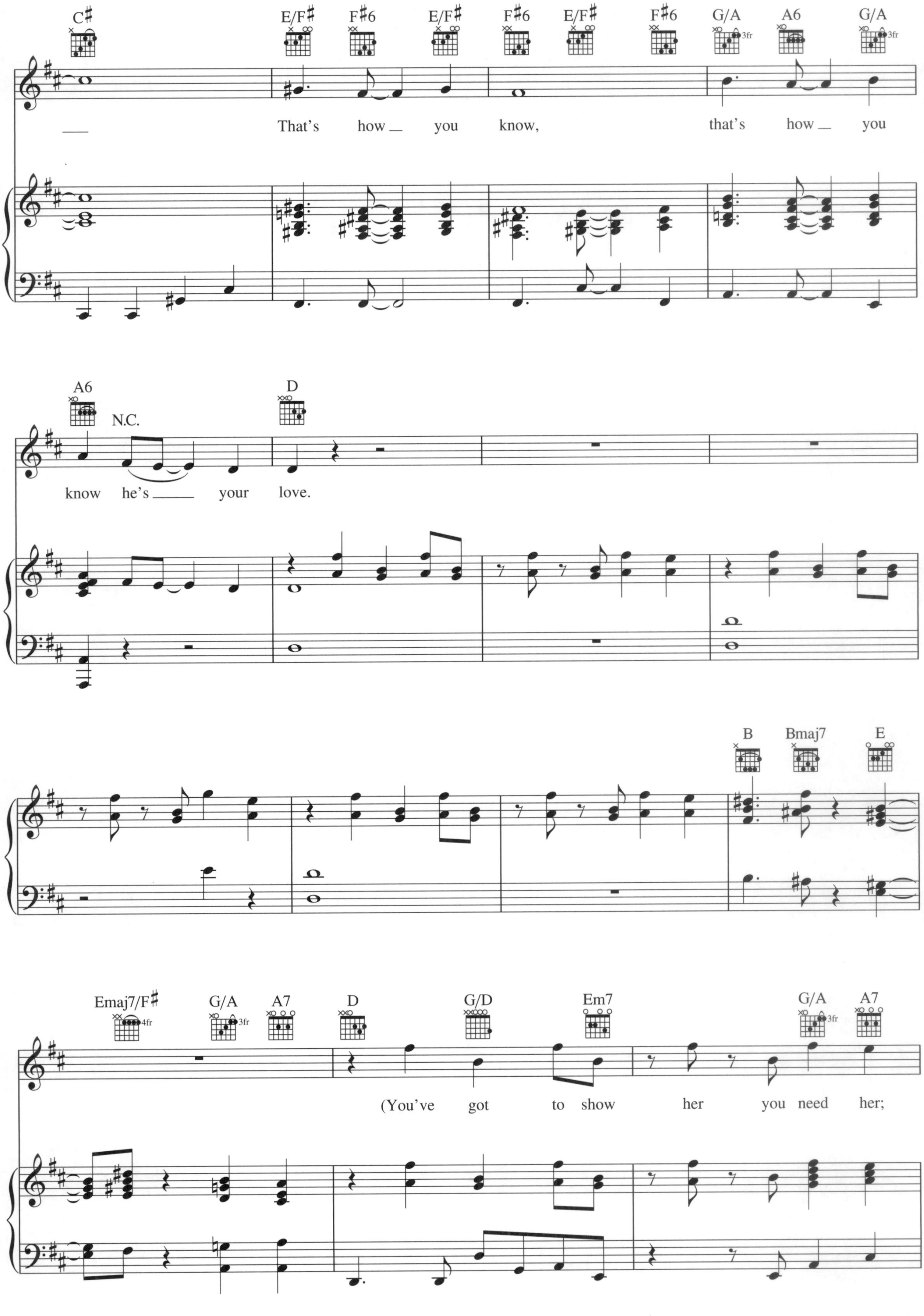

C♯ E/F♯ F♯6 E/F♯ F♯6 E/F♯ F♯6 G/A A6 G/A

___ That's how ___ you know, that's how ___ you

A6 N.C. D

know he's ___ your love.

B Bmaj7 E

Emaj7/F♯ G/A A7 D G/D Em7 G/A A7

(You've got to show her you need her;

D
G/D
Em7
G/A
A7
3fr
don't treat her like a mind - read - er! Each day do some -
thing to lead her to be - lieve you love her.)
F♯7sus
F♯7
B
B/D♯
4fr
E
Emaj7/G♯
Ev - 'ry - bod - y wants to live hap - pi - ly ev - er af - ter.
(You've got to show her you need her.)
G
Ev - 'ry - bod - y wants to know their true love is

B
B/D♯
E
Emaj7/G♯
G/A
A7
D
G/D
Em7
G/A
A7
true. How do you know he
(How does she know that you love her?
D
G/D
Em7
G/A
A7
D
G/D
loves you? How do you know
How do you show her you love her? How does she know
F♯7sus
F♯7
B
B/D♯
G♯m
B
E
F♯
he's yours? Well, does he
that you real - ly, real - ly, tru - ly...)
B
B/D♯
E
C♯m7
take you out danc - ing just so he can hold you close?

C♯m7/F♯
F♯7
B
B/D♯
E
Ded - i - cate a song with words meant just for
C♯m7
C♯m7/F♯
F♯7
D♯m
you? Ooh.
He'll find his own way to
G♯m
B/C♯
C♯
E/F♯
F♯6
E/F♯
tell you with the lit - tle things he'll do.
That's how you
F♯6
E/F♯
F♯6
G/A
A6
G/A
A7sus
N.C.
know, that's how you know he's your love.

B
B/D♯
E
Emaj7/G♯
G/A
A7
D
G/D
Em7
That's how you know
(La la la la
he loves you.
la la la la, la la la la la la la la.
That's how you know
F♯7sus
F♯7
G♯m
it's true.
La la la la la la la la la la la

B
E
F♯
B
B/D♯
4fr
E
Be - cause he'll wear your fav - 'rite col - or just so he can
la la.)
C♯m7
4fr
C♯m7/F♯
9fr
F♯7
B
B/D♯
4fr
match your eyes;
plan a pri - vate pic - nic
E
C♯m7
4fr
C♯m7/F♯
9fr
F♯7
by the fi - re's glow,
oh.
D♯m
6fr
G♯m
4fr
B/C♯
His heart - 'll be yours for - ev - er,
some-thing ev - 'ry day will

C♯
E/F♯
F♯6
E/F♯
F♯6
E/F♯
F♯6
show. That's how you know,
(That's how you
G/A
A6
G/A
A6
E/F♯
F♯6
E/F♯
F♯6
E/F♯
F♯6
that's how you know, That's how you know,
know, that's how you know, that's how you
G/A
A6
G/A
1 A6
2 Gmaj7/A
3fr
2fr
N.C.
that's how you know. know he's your love.
know, that's how you know...) (That's how she knows
that you love her. That's how you show her you love her.
That's how you

D
G
A
know,
You've got to show her you need her; don't treat her like
G/A
A7
G/D
Em7
that's how you know
a mind - read - er!) (How do you know that you love her?
he's your love.
That's how you know that you love her. It's not e - nough to take
Em/D
the one you love for grant - ed!

THIS IS ME

from the Disney Channel Original Movie CAMP ROCK

Words and Music by ADAM WATTS
and ANDY DODD

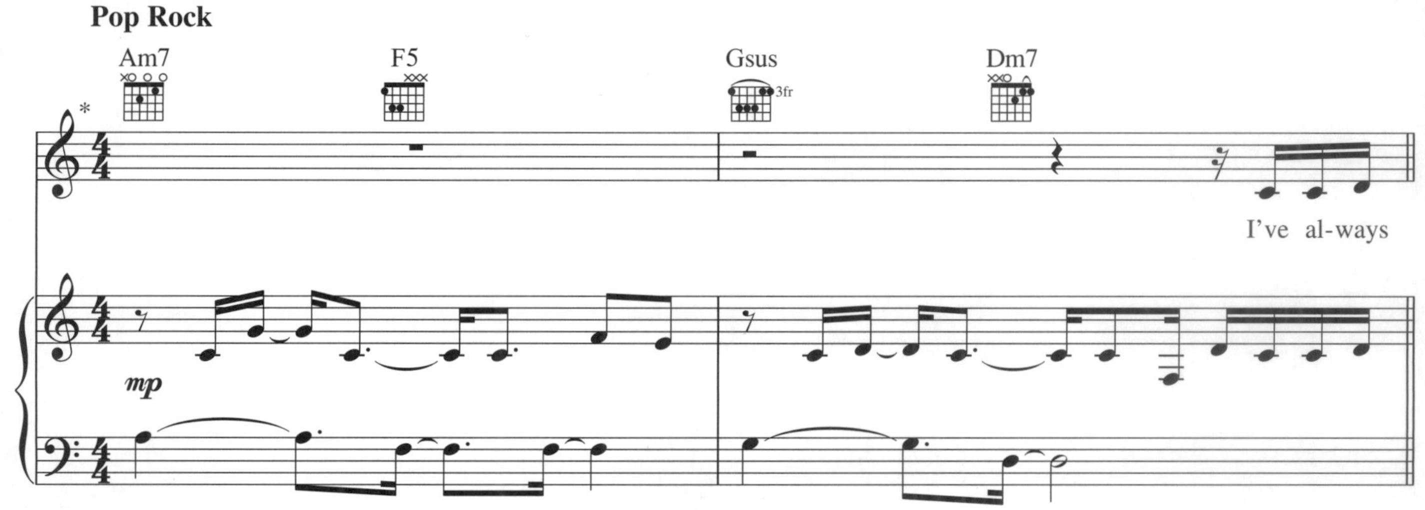

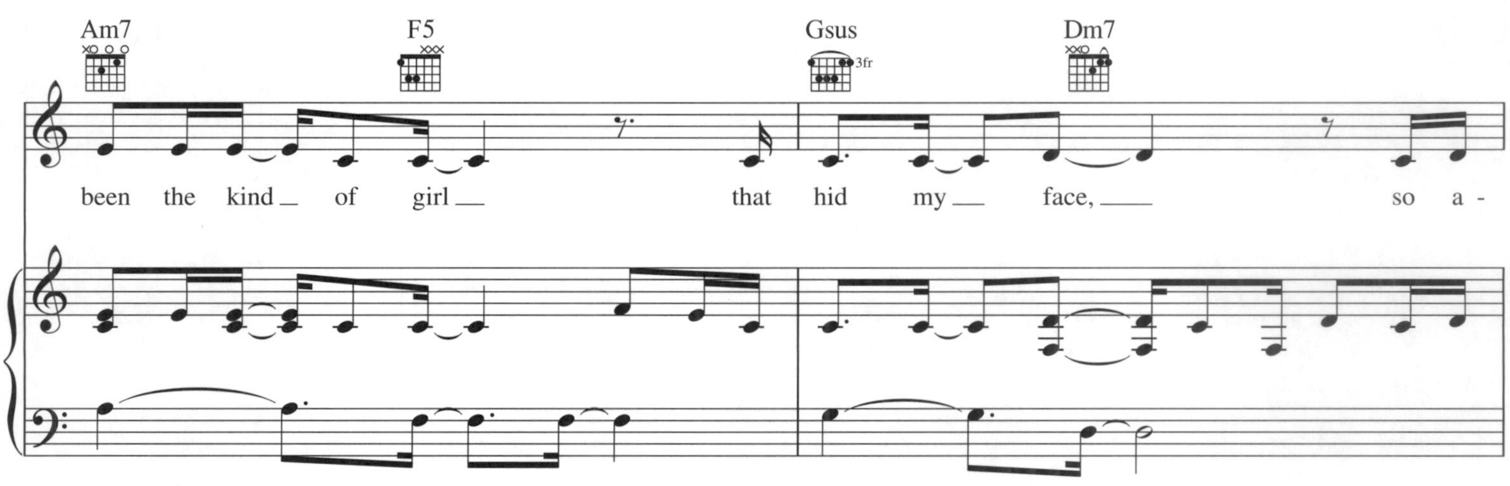

* Recorded a half step higher.

Am
F
C
Dm
have this dream bright in - side of me, I'm gon - na
let it show. It's time to let you know, to let you know.
G
This is real, this is me, I'm ex - act -
- ly where I'm sup - posed to be, now. Gon - na let the light

G
Am
F
shine on me. Now I've found who I am, there's no
C
G
Dm7
To Coda
way to hold it in. No more hid - ing who I want to be,
F
G
Am7
F5
C
G5
3fr
C5
3fr
this is me. Do you
Am
F
C
Dm
know what it's like to feel so in the dark, to

Am
F
C
Dm
dream a - bout a life where you're the shin - ing star? E - ven
though it seems like it's too far a - way, I
have to be - lieve in my - self. It's the on - ly way.
D.S. al Coda
G
This is
CODA
this is

Am F C Dm Am F

me.

G F C

You're the voice I hear inside my head, the

G F C

reason that I'm singing. I need to find you, I've got to find

G Am7 F C

you. You're the miss - ing piece I need, the song

G
Am7
Dm
inside of me. I need to find you, I've got to find
G
F
C
you. This is real, this is me, I'm exact-
G
Am
F
C
ly where I'm supposed to be, now. Gonna let the light
G
Am
F
shine on me. Now I've found who I am, there's no

C
G
Dm7
way to hold it in.
No more hid - ing who I want to be,

F
G
F
C
this is me.
You're the miss - ing piece I need, the song

Gsus
3fr
G
F
C
in - side of me. You're the voice I hear in - side my head, the

Gsus
3fr
Am
F
C
rea - son that _ I'm sing - ing. Now I've found ___ who I am, ___ there's no

G
Dm7
way to hold ______ it in. _________ No more hid - ing who I want to be, _

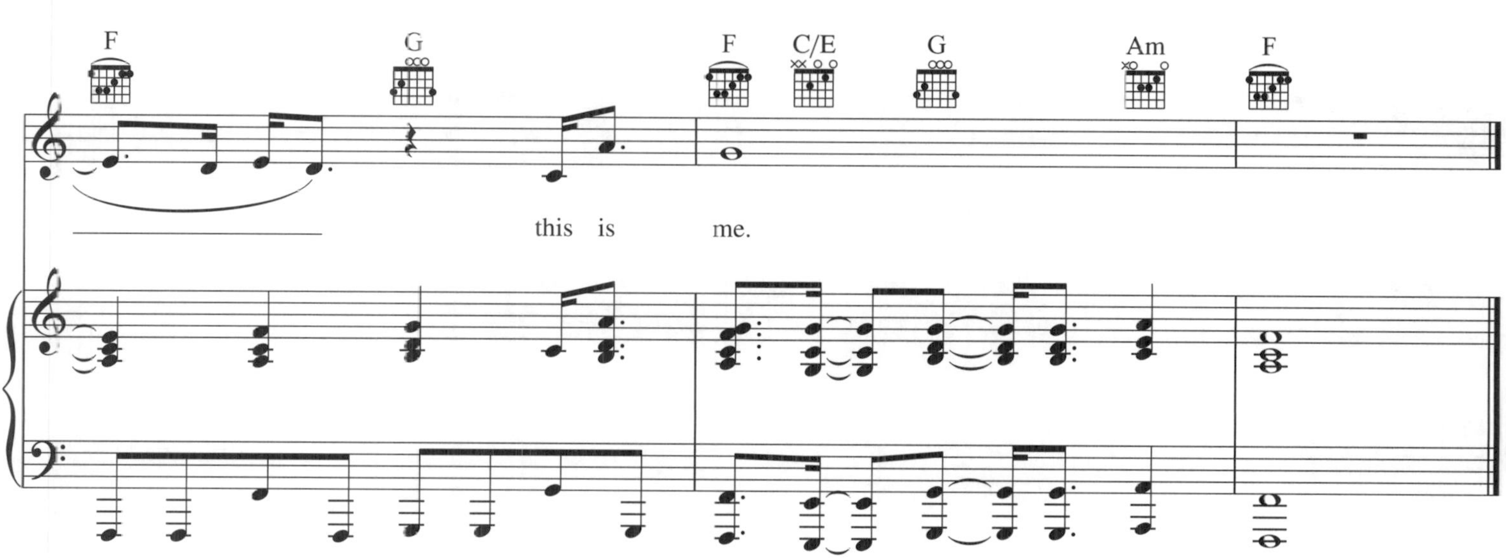

F
G
F
C/E
G
Am
F
this is me.

UPSIDE DOWN

from the Universal Pictures and Imagine Entertainment film CURIOUS GEORGE

Words and Music by
JACK JOHNSON

E
each new day
I can feel a change in
F♯m
ev - 'ry - thing.
And as the sur - face breaks, re -
E
flec - tions fade.
Who's to say
But in some ways they re -
I can't do ev - 'ry - thing? Well,
F♯m
main the same.
I can try.
And as my mind be - gins to
And as I roll a - long I be -

E
spread its wings,
gin to find
there's no stop - ping cu - ri -
things aren't al - ways just
F♯m
os - i - ty.
what they seem.
I wan - na turn the whole thing
E
F♯m
A
B
up - side down.
I'll find the things they say just
E
F♯m
A
B
can't be found.
I'll share this love I find with

E
F♯m
A
B
ev - 'ry - one.
We'll sing and dance to Moth - er
To Coda
Na - ture's songs.
I don't want this feel - in' to go a - way.
E
F♯m7
3

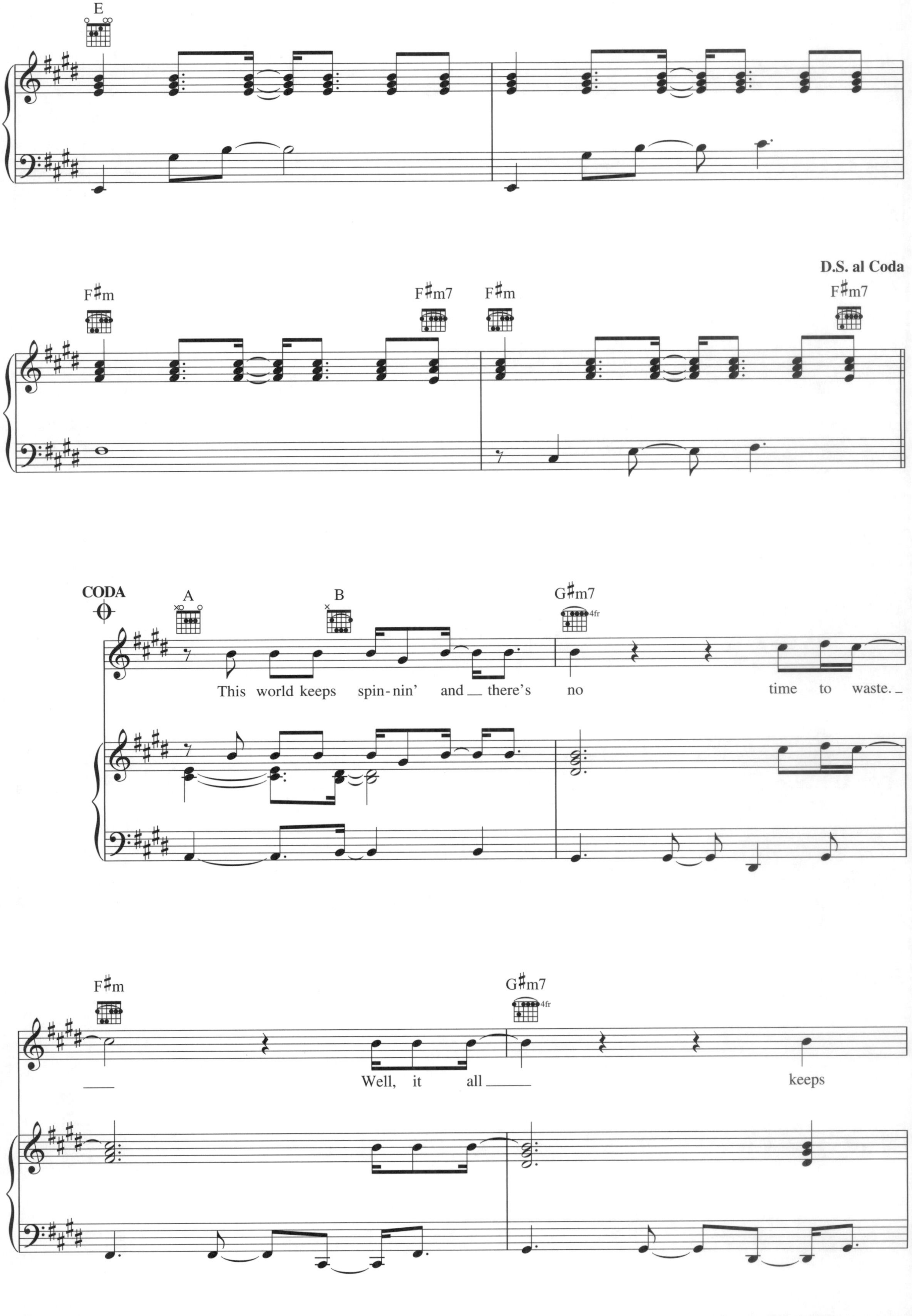

E

F♯m F♯m7 F♯m

D.S. al Coda

F♯m7

CODA

A B G♯m7

This world keeps spin-nin' and __ there's no time to waste. _

A
B
E
F♯m
spin - nin', spin - nin', round and round and up - side down.
Who's to say what's im - pos - si - ble and can't be found?
I don't want this feel - in' to go a - way.
(Vocal 1st time only)
Please don't go a - way.
3

E
F♯m
Please don't go a - way.
E
F♯m
A
F♯m
Is this how it's sup - posed to be?
rit.
E
F♯m
A
E
Is this how it's sup - posed to be?

YOU ARE THE MUSIC IN ME

from the Disney Channel Original Movie HIGH SCHOOL MUSICAL 2

Words and Music by
JAMIE HOUSTON

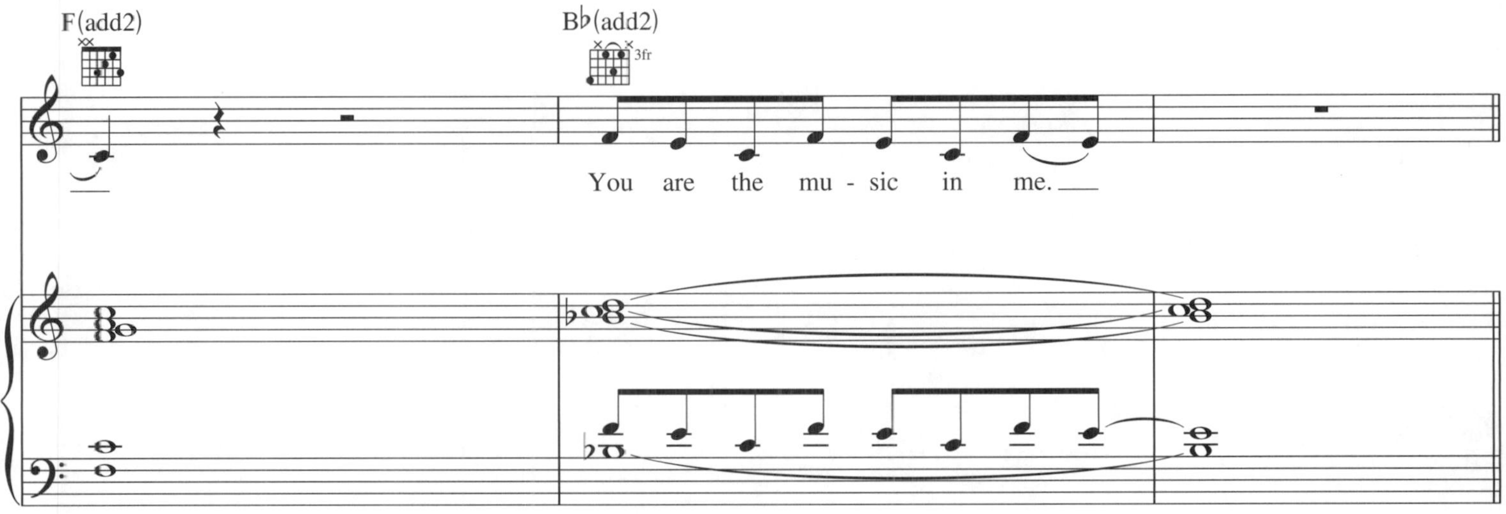

B♭
F
- ten. There's a rea - son.
C
Kelsi & Gabriella:
When you dream, there's a chance you'll find a lit - tle laugh -
B♭
F
C/E
Dm
- ter or "hap - py ev - er af - ter." You're a har - mo - ny to the
Gabriella & Troy:
C/E
F
C/E
mel - o - dy that's ech - o - ing in - side my head. A sin -
Gabriella:

Dm
C/E
B♭
-gle voice above the noise, and like a com-mon thread,
G/T:
C
B♭6
Troy: mmm, you're pull-ing me.
Gabriella: When I hear my fav-'rite song, I know that we
F
B♭(add2)
3fr
be-long.
Troy: Oh, you are the mu-sic in me.
C
B♭6
Yeah, it's liv-ing in all of us,
Gabriella: and it's brought us here

F
B♭(add2)
3fr
C
be - cause
Troy & Gabriella: you are the mu - sic in me.
All: Na, na, na, na,
B♭6
F
B♭
na, na, na, na, na,
na, na, na, na.
T/G: You are the mu - sic in me.
F(add2)
C
B♭
Gabriella:
It's like I knew you be - fore we met.
Can't ex - plain,
there's no name
F
C
for it.
T/G: I sang you words I've nev - er said,
Troy: and it was

B♭
F
C/E
Dm
eas - y, be-cause you see the real me. As I Both: am you un-
C/E
F
- der - stand, and that's more than I've ev -
C/E
Dm
C/E
- er known. Gabriella: To hear your voice a - bove the noise, Both: and
B♭
know I'm not a - lone. Gabriella: Oh, you're sing - in' to me.

C
Bb6
Both: When I hear my fav - 'rite song, I know that we
F
Bb(add2)
3fr
be - long. You are the mu - sic in me.
C
Bb6
It's liv - in' in all of us, and it's brought us here
F
Bb(add2)
3fr
be - cause you are the mu - sic in me.

Dm7
C/E
(Me.) To - geth - er we're gon - na sing. (Sing.)
B♭maj9
We got the pow - er to say what we feel,
Troy: con -
nect - ed and real,
Gabriella: can't keep it all in - side.
C
B♭6
F
All: (Na, na, na, na.) (Na, na, na, na, na.) (Na, na, na, na. You

B♭
C
B♭6
are the mu - sic in me.)
(Na, na, na, na.)
(Na, na, na, na, na.)
F
B♭
(Na, na, na, na. You are the mu - sic in me.)
C
B♭6
All: When I hear my fav - 'rite song, I know that we
(Lead vocals ad lib. to end)
F
B♭(add2)
3fr
be - long. You are the mu - sic in me.

C
B♭/D
It's liv - in' in all of us, and it's brought us here
F
B♭(add2)
3fr
be - cause you are the mu - sic in me.
C
B♭
F
Na, na, na, na. Na, na, na, na, na. Na, na, na, na. You
B♭
C/B♭
are the mu - sic in me.

150 of the Most Beautiful Songs Ever

The Best Acoustic Rock Songs Ever

The Best Children's Songs Ever

The Best Contemporary Christian Songs Ever
Contemporary Christian

The Best Early Rock 'n' Roll Songs Ever

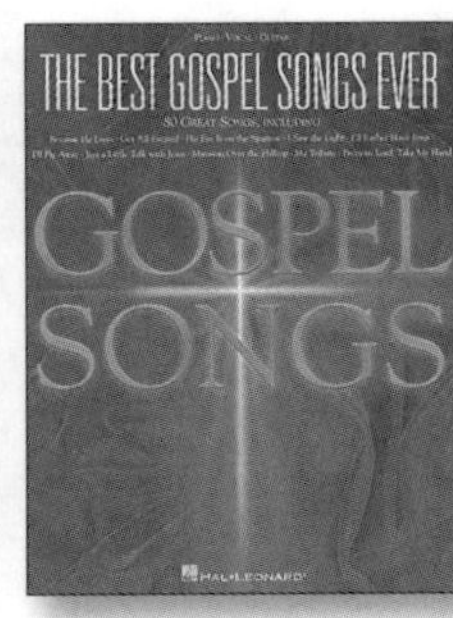
The Best Gospel Songs Ever
Gospel Songs

The Best Songs Ever
Best Songs Ever

The Best Torch Songs Ever
Torch Songs

The Best TV Songs Ever

HAL•LEONARD®
CORPORATION